TAKING FULL MEASURE

'TAKING FULL MEASURE /

Rethinking Assessment Through the Arts

Robert Orrill, Executive Editor

Dennie (Palmer) Wolf
Nancy Pistone

College Entrance Examination Board, New York, 1995

Dennie Palmer Wolf is Director, PACE (Performance Assessment Collaborative for Education), Cambridge, Massachusetts.

Nancy Pistone is an arts education consultant and former Supervisor of Visual Arts, Pittsburgh Public Schools, Pennsylvania.

Robert Orrill is Executive Director of the Office of Academic Affairs, the College Board, New York.

The following publishers have kindly given permission to use quotations from copyrighted works.

Page 6: From "Maintenance and Extension of Traditions," by Dr. Tomás Ybarra-Frausto. Reprinted with permission of the Mexican Museum, San Francisco, California, from its 1986 exhibition catalog *Lo del Corazón: Heartbeat of a Culture*.

Pages 7 and 33: From *Private Domain*, by Paul Taylor. Copyright © 1987. Reprinted by permission of Alfred A. Knopf.

Pages 20 and 21: From *The Member of the Wedding*, by Carson McCullers. Copyright © 1949 by Carson McCullers. Reprinted by permission of New Directions Publishing Corporation.

Pages 34, 37, and 38-40: From "Both Artist and Instrument: An Approach to Dance Education," by Martha Barylick. Reprinted by permission of *Dœdalus*, Journal of the American Academy of Arts and Sciences, Summer 1983, vòl. 112, no. 3.

The College Board is a national nonprofit association that champions educational excellence for all students through the ongoing collaboration of more than 2,900 member schools, colleges, universities, education systems, and associations. The Board promotes—by means of responsive forums, research, programs, and policy development—universal access to high standards of learning, equality of opportunity, and sufficient financial support so that every student is prepared for success in college and work.

Some of the work described here was funded in part by the Rockefeller Foundation, through its funding of ARTS PROPEL, a project of CHART (Collaborative for Humanities and Art Teaching) programs. The project is the outcome of a collaboration between Project Zero, Harvard Graduate School of Education; Educational Testing Service; and the Pittsburgh Public Schools. During the 10-year period of the College Board's Educational EQuality Project, the Thinking Series was initiated. *Taking Full Measure* is the fourth title in this series and is an outgrowth of the project.

Researchers are encouraged to express freely their professional judgment. Therefore, points of view or opinions stated in College Board books do not necessarily represent official College Board position or policy.

Single copies of *Taking Full Measure* can be purchased for $12.00. Payment or purchase order should be addressed to: College Board Publications, Box 886, New York, New York 10101-0886.

Library of Congress Catalog Number: 91-072568
ISBN: 0-87447-539-2

Printed in the United States of America

Contents

Foreword

T *aking Full Measure* is another in the Thinking Series of publications initiated by the College Board's Educational EQuality Project—a 10-year effort to improve the quality of secondary education and to ensure equal access to college for all students. The books in this series address what many observers recognize as the central problem in significant educational change: the work of teaching all students, not a few, how to become competent thinkers (Resnick and Klopfer 1989). This work brings into existence a new conception of the place of thinking in the high school curriculum. Rather than being treated as a special, separate, and final skill, thinking becomes the substance of the most basic classroom activities for all students in all subject areas. This series is designed to convey through discussion and example how many teachers are already making this new conception a reality in their classrooms—how, that is, they make even ordinary moments occasions of thought for their students.

Taking Full Measure examines how arts teachers use varied and progressive approaches to enhance the thinking skills of their students. In so doing, these teachers help students turn information into inspiration, and emphasize sustained work and reflection rather than cramming and rote recall. Other books in this series address thinking in history, mathematics, science and foreign language. Each explores how immersion in knowledge is required for thinking. All of the books, however, draw on both cognitive research and actual instances of classroom practice to convey how thinking should not be an activity that comes late in the curriculum after the acquisition of content, but rather is integral to successful learning in even the most commonplace and basic classroom situations. With deliberate purpose, *Taking Full Measure* and the other books in this series constitute a response to what Lauren Resnick has described as the urgent need "to take seriously the aspiration of making thinking . . . a regular part of a school program for all the population, even minorities, even non-English speakers, even the poor" (Resnick 1987).

ROBERT ORRILL
OFFICE OF ACADEMIC AFFAIRS
THE COLLEGE BOARD

Acknowledgments

T his book is the result of a diverse collaboration among teachers and researchers working in a range of artistic disciplines. The authors, Dennie Wolf and Nancy Pistone, wish to thank the following contributors:

Contributing Authors

Larry Scripp, instructor, New England Conservatory of Music, Boston, Massachusetts

Steve Seidel, Harvard Graduate School of Education, Cambridge, Massachusetts

Rieneke Zessoules, Harvard Graduate School of Education, Cambridge, Massachusetts.

Collaborating Teachers and Artists

Martha Armstrong-Gray, dance teacher, Cambridge School of Weston, Weston, Massachusetts

Walter Askin, professor of art, California State University at Los Angeles, California

Martha Barylick, dance teacher, Mamaroneck High School, Mamaroneck, New York

Beverly Bates, art teacher, CAPA High School, Pittsburgh, Pennsylvania

Norman Brown, art teacher, Schenley High School, Pittsburgh Public Schools, Pennsylvania

Mary Burger, poet, Boston University Creative Writing Program, Boston, Massachusetts

Lyle Davidson, chairman, Theory Department, New England Conservatory of Music, Boston, Massachusetts

Barbara Erlich, dance teacher, Cambridge Rindge and Latin High School, Cambridge, Massachusetts

Jerry Halpern, English teacher, Langley High School, Pittsburgh Public Schools, Pennsylvania

Cynthia Katz, photography teacher, Concord Academy, Concord, Massachusetts

Johnathan Levy, professor of drama, State University of New York at Stony Brook, New York

Amalia Mesa-Bains, artist, San Francisco, California

Carolyn Olasewere, English teacher, Westinghouse High School, Pittsburgh Public Schools, Pennsylvania

Karen Price, art teacher, Schenley High School, Pittsburgh, Pennsylvania

Linda Ross-Broadus, choral music teacher, Westinghouse High School, Pittsburgh Public Schools, Pennsylvania

Nanette Seago, mathematics teacher, Mission Middle School, Riverside, California

Tony Spears, mathematics coordinator, California Mathematics Project, San Diego County Office, San Diego, California

Arts Academic Advisory Committee 1990–91

Walter Askin, Professor of Art, California State University–Los Angeles, Los Angeles, California

E. Frank Bluestein, Chairman of Department of Fine Arts, Germantown High School, Germantown, Tennesee

Rosann McLaughin Cox, Dance Department Coordinator, Arts, Arts Magnet High School, Dallas, Texas

Nicolas Kanellos, Professor, Department of Hispanic and Classical Languages, University of Houston, Houston, Texas

Nancy Pistone, Former Supervisor of Visual Arts, Pittsburgh Public Schools, Pittsburgh, Pennsylvania

Dolleye M. E. Robinson, Assistant Dean, School of Liberal Arts, Professor of Music, Jackson State University, Jackson, Missouri

Gary Wolfman, Director of Orchestras, Appleton Public High Schools, Appleton, Wisconsin

CHAPTER 1

Introduction: The Work of Art

I f you open any educational report to its first page you will find a challenge to educators to teach all students higher-order thinking skills. The consensus is striking and the imperative is strong. But exactly what is meant by this now nearly magical phrase, "higher-order thinking skills"? The answers have grown almost as familiar as a times table or a string of state capitals: "Problem-solving, reasoning, synthesis...." But if we are seeking a robust view of thinking, perhaps we don't want such a settled educational catechism.

In most views of learning, philosophers, scientists, and historians "think," while carpenters, mothers, and actors only "do." The real materials of learning are taken to be words, logic, and formulae, not wood, bread, or lives. But suppose for a moment that we let go of those comfortable presuppositions. What would happen to the notion of higher or critical thinking, for instance, if we took the work of artists—making and performing—as forms of thought?

Stepping Back to Look

If late last year you walked into the Los Angeles County Museum and made your way to the galleries hung with Chicano art, sooner or later you would have met a large installation, *Emblems of the Decade: Numbers and Borders,* by Amalia Mesa-Bains in collaboration with Victor Zamudio-Taylor. Part image, part sculpture, part thought, it commands attention.

An intricate display, its two halves inscribe the richness and the harshness of Latino life. On one side of the long room, its many numbers are the harsh statistics that give an account of contemporary American life as lived by people of Spanish

Emblems of the Decade: Numbers

and Indian descent: Incomes that hover or fall below the amount that marks off poverty from survival; the increasing slope that graphs the numbers of AIDS patients; the rising population of illegal entrants seeking a new life that they will live covertly. These statistics mix with the dates of conquest, annexation, liberation, and independence: 1898 and 1910. The recurrent presence of counting devices and demographic inscriptions suggests the larger, quantitative culture that looms behind, collecting, tabulating, and comparing lives. But cropping up between these dark quantities are magical and spiritual numbers: Tokens of hope, luck, wonder, and belief. Across the room

Emblems of the Decade: Borders

is its companion installation, bearing the title *Borders*. Icons about living at the literal and imagined edge line the top of a wooden bureau and crowd its feet. These emblems are those of immigration: the dresser, the suitcase, the rusted truck with

Emblems of the Decade: Detail of Borders

its dark earth. On the wall above are the emblems of separated lives: photographs and letters. Like some great Mayan calendar, the two facing wholes insist on the seasons and faces of Latino culture—the overwhelming poverty of many, their mar-

Altar

Altar

TAKING FULL MEASURE

ginal and illegal lives bound together and enriched with magic, blood ties, and spirituality.

This is what a viewer can see if he or she waits and looks closely. But what is invisible is the wide history and long evolution of thought that underlies *Emblems*. In Amalia Mesa-Bains's family kitchen there was always an altar to household saints and to family history. In her community, she renewed the *ofrenda* each year on El Dia de los Muertos, when the souls of the dead return to be honored, with carefully arranged displays of food, household objects, and mementos. As a young woman, Mesa-Bains learned the significance of folk forms from family artisans. Later, as an artist, she built altars in her community that went past practice to become sculpture. While the form of the altar remained constant, its sizes and shapes, the saints invoked, and the messages carried have shifted.

But *Emblems* is more than a personal memento. Its icons play with the sixteenth- and seventeenth-century Hispanic tradition of emblems: highly symbolic images made by pairing titles, commentary, and vivid images. But rather than spiritual or literary signs, Mesa-Bains has assembled political and social commentary. In the end, the numbers and border signs Mesa-Bains uses are laminates—they draw on memory, the enduring icons of Latino and Hispanic culture, and her own critical sense of what must be said. In so doing, *Emblems of the Decade* brings together the lovely and the unbearable—elegant forms and difficult messages, not unlike the murals of Jose Clemente Orozeo and Diego Rivera, or Sebastiao Salgado's photographs of farm workers and miners. It documents the diversity of the human present without bleaching, denying, or condensing it, much as quilts and pulled-thread coverlets record Appalachian women's lives, or field songs document the will to make images and music even under the condition of slavery. The result is a set of inscriptions written in the thickest of languages: sensual, symbolic, and deeply cultural. As Tomás Ybarra-Frausto, a scholar of Hispanic culture, writes:

In ancient times, it was the task of the artist to "deify

things," to reveal through form, color, and line the inherent divinity in all earthly things. Across time and space, the moral dimension of the artist has been maintained. Today, an aesthetic obligation and major duty of the artist continues to be to produce art with a heartfelt intuition— *hacer las cosas con corazón.* While the artistic mind explores and depicts the deep structures of social reality, it is the higher task of the heart to intuit and express the boundless horizons of the imagination (Ybarra-Frausto 1986, 13).

But there is still another kind of thought here. The sketches

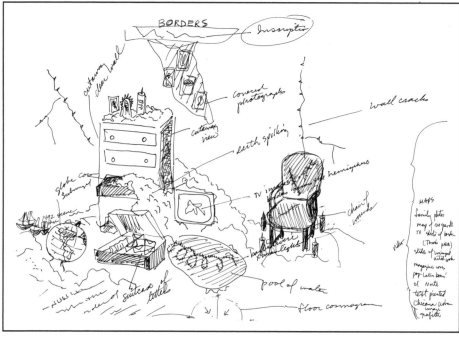

Emblems of the Decade: Preliminary sketch of Borders

that litter Mesa-Bains's studio show that a work like *Emblems* is a network of hard and careful choices: To cut away the side of the dresser rather than leave it closed; to "wound" the wall and chair upholstery; to fuse the imagery of barbed wire and Christmas lights. Without the ability to pursue such choices, *Emblems* might have been thin, plain, even mild.

While the museum catalog describes *Emblems* as a multi-media work made from photos, letters, paint, and wood, in truth, it is made—at least as much—from pauses, from moving an image or object from here to there, from stepping back to look, from calling in others to play the critic. The work has an invisible ingredient—a constant, almost ruthless assessment.

Here is how turning to the arts breaks open the definition of "thinking." Critique and assessment are not afterwords but absolute ingredients of thought. At their best, arts classrooms are cultures built around the question, "Is this good enough—yet?" It is that capacity that dancer and choreographer Paul Taylor touches on in remembering an evening when at last he saw one of his most acclaimed dances, "Aureole," in performance:

> After the premiere, critics write that "Aureole" typifies just about everything that modern dance has been trying to do away with. Allen Hughes of the *New York Times* says it's "different, daring, and delightful."
>
> "Delightful." Who was I was to argue with the *Times*? Yet there's something. . . . If I could only duplicate myself and send one of me out front to see what it looks like.
>
> Later on, when out with an injury, I was able to see it, and my nagging doubts were confirmed. The dance had been good to me. I appreciated it, valued and trusted it, but was out of sympathy. Though I understood its audience appeal, for me it had little. I too enjoyed seeing dances that required little effort to understand, ones that gave uplift and caused a smile. Yet I was not smiling. I couldn't forget how relatively easy the dance had been to make and how previous dances, both larger and smaller scaled, had stretched my goals much further. "Aureole" had been child's play compared with others that I had had to dig for, grapple with, and slave over, ones that had a more developed craft to them but weren't as popular. It was impossible to know if it would continue to be appreciated: yet for all its success, perhaps because of it, "Aureole" filled me with resentment. I was wary of it. It caused me to see a time coming when a choice would have to be made—to remain on the comfortably safe side of the doorway to success, or to pass through it and into a tougher and a lot less familiar place (Taylor 1987, 140–1).

Assessment as an Episode of Learning

The term "student assessment" usually provokes images of heads bent over short-answer questions or problem sets. However, in the following essay, we observe teachers and their students making assessment part of learning to think critically. What their examples offer us—and this applies to teachers of history, mathematics, and science, as well as those in the arts—is generous and alerting, given the usual dogged beliefs about assessment. These teachers and students argue that, at its core, assessment ought to involve the following:

- *An insistence on excellence:* Arts classes are full of talk about what's good; they also foster expectations of excellence. The talk is not just of high standards but of those still being invented. Teachers openly discuss what they expect of students. From the outset, and recurrently, they insist not just on completeness, or neatness, or technique, but on risk, invention, and investigation.

- *Judgment:* There is much about art work that simply will not submit to measurement based on notions of single correct answers. A painting, or a new performance of Lorraine Hansberry's "Les Blancs," ought to provoke a chorus of opinions about a range of qualitative issues—wisdom, insight, handsomeness, craft, and moral choice.

- *The importance of self-assessment:* No artist survives without being what the artist Ben Shahn calls "the spontaneous imaginer and the inexorable critic." An episode of assessment should be an occasion when students learn to read and appraise their own work.

- *The use of multiple forms of assessment:* In many studios and practice rooms teachers use varied forms of assessment—everyday conversation and comments, critiques and reviews—as preparation for more finished and higher-stakes performances and exhibitions. Each is a tool honed to its particular purposes.

- *Ongoing assessment:* Wise assessment is continuous, it does not jump up, like a jack-in-the-box, at the end of a term or a year. Because it is ongoing, this continuous kind of assessment permits students to reflect on their own performance and to plow back the criticism into their work.

In this light, assessment is not so much a test as an episode of learning. These students and teachers argue that a major, perhaps the primary, reason for assessment is to teach students how to be rigorous critics of their own work, and to have what editor and writer Ted Solotaroff calls "a few good voices" in their heads. ■

CHAPTER 2

Making the Invisible Seen: Making Excellence Public

eter Payson, a college photography teacher, describes what he looks for in a photograph:

> Look at the catalog from the college where I teach. Open it to the description of the portfolio you have to submit to get into the photography program. The details are all there; at least eight pieces, no larger than 11" x 14", nothing framed, hand-coloring and cropping of images is allowed. But there is not one word—not one—about the heart of the matter: what makes the body of work worth looking at. That's invisible. But I'll tell you what I look for—a portfolio where the images shout, "I have a sense for what good work is."

It's Tuesday, early in the semester, one of the first "crit" sessions in a high school Photo II class. A teacher, Cynthia Katz, walks up and down past the ranks of contact sheets and working prints; her students do the same. It's tough, quiet work. The prints are rough, some scratched, some utterly dark, some washed white. Seeing what they might have to offer takes concentration. Katz turns and talks to her students:

> What am I looking for? Some technical things. You know I'm a stickler for craft. I'm looking to see that consistency of exposure. Sure, I want to know, "Can you use that incredibly dumb and necessary tool, the light meter?"
>
> But I am really looking for other things. I want to know, *"Can you investigate yet?"* I told you to shoot a roll of film for your project. Some of you came in moaning, "Oh, I wasn't able to finish . . . I could only find 24 pictures."
>
> I said, "You've got 12 exposures left? Get to know that stool over there. Find something that interests you about it, and investigate it."

The world is not full of perfect pictures waiting to be snapped. You have to flush them out of the bushes; you find them, you wait for the light, the head tilt, the birds to take off. You walk up closer, you go find the white pitcher and put it on the table for contrast. I'm looking for the contact sheet that's 36 exposures, all hunting down an idea.

And I'm looking for selectivity. I look at your contact sheets for what you circled with that wax crayon. I want to know, when you look over those rows and columns of images, what do you go for? Is it just the neat and clean picture, or can you see something quirky, unexpected, something that, if you worked on it, would become a strong image?

And I'm looking for pursuit. What a word! But it's what I mean. When you go in and make a rough print and then a refined print, is there something there that's coming into focus? I don't mean just technically. Are all the tools you've got—the filters, the paper, the printing, the framing, the contrast—lining up over something?

I mean, are you seeing something that wasn't just plunked in front of the camera? Are you seeing into something, and are you going to keep after it?

Katz could have written up a sheet that listed the requirements for the assignment: 36 exposures, all of the same subject; a contact sheet with the three best images circled; one of those images printed; and the test strip for that image. She could have mimeographed the sheet, and students would cram it somewhere into a biology book or put it in the bottom of a locker. But she is talking standards, not requirements. "What is the point of giving them just the list and leaving them to discover what really matters? Why hide out? Go public."

With this as introduction, Katz and her students enter a series of long-term assignments—Self-Portrait, Landscape. Each is a project in itself that includes looking at slides, talking about the visual qualities and ideas in those images, shooting rolls of film, developing contact sheets, studying and selecting from the contacts, making rough, exploratory prints, taking part in "crits" of work in progress, and developing finished prints. Throughout this process the students keep a portfolio of their work from which they are expected to develop a project of their own that shows their development in each area.

As a reprise, Katz talks to her students about photographers whose work she thinks will enable them—literally—to see "investigation." In class, she throws nonstop images onto the white wall—all to give a sense of how an individual sensibility becomes a curiosity, and then a vision, and, finally, a body of compelling visual exploration. Today, she holds up Catherine Wagner's recently published book, *American Classrooms*. She displays the glossy pages of photos that show the steely order of a classroom at NASA, the clutter of a beautician's school, a science lab where a molecular model dwarfs the chairs.

> This is a project. It has a core, an idea that the photographer wanted to investigate, not just one photo that she wanted to make over and over in different locations. She wanted to show us the kind of place a classroom is, how it trains our attention, how its furniture structures relationships, how it teaches. But, like all projects, the vision emerged gradually. I don't think that when Catherine Wagner began she knew what or how she was going to investigate. That evolved. She started photographing something that compelled her, and it grew. That's the method: Find something that interests you, don't abandon it, explore it, make it evolve.

Learning to Investigate

Evolution is not magic. And learning to investigate is work that demands *ongoing*, not final, assessment. Comments and in-class talk are two daily, ongoing forms of assessment. The comments are scrawled notes attached to the images that students submit weekly in big manila envelopes. These comments are short, but they are meant to provoke. They are meant to "nag" students into doing more than just snapping a roll of easy "candids." Katz gives this example:

> How do the comments work? Take Lee's work. When I looked at her portfolio at the end of the first semester I could see possibilities for the first time. She had made a

series of zoo photos, with the animals caught tight in their cages. And a very strange photo of a squirrel mowed flat on a road. There was a dry sense of humor, a sense of the bizarre shaping up. I wrote her a note, clipped it to the

> Lee —
> Images in driveway — w/ you in foreground + Dad in 'back', Smiling, waving, are quite funny — the juxtaposition of you two creates a wonderful irony — + is strong. The setting is new too — suburbs, home, neighborhood, family — pursue this! More! Good job.

squirrel, and told her not to dismiss the images as jokes but to push them.

A while ago I was looking at her contact sheets again. There was a new line of work, clearly about women's place in life. But I am waiting to see if that's what she makes of it. There were a lot of images with herself in the foreground doing very dramatic things, close up to the camera. Her father was in the background, calmly waving, watering the yard. I wrote her another note, picking out these images as new and interesting. She never wrote back. But the next set of contacts that came in showed that she had pushed the strange, staged quality of the images by moving them inside where the curtains and coffee mugs made them seem even more bizarre.

The talk about how to investigate an idea visually also goes on, out loud, in various kinds of studio conversations. What happens is often telegraphic, but pointed. Several weeks later,

Katz moves about the studio, among students hunched over recent contact sheets. She stops to lean over Lee's shoulder. Together they scan the rows and columns of images that continue to picture half-comic, half-dangerous domestic scenes.

Katz: Which ones are you thinking of printing?

Lee: These. *[She points to two strange, constructed images of a man nonchalantly reading a newspaper, a coffee cup held aloft, seated offhandedly on the broad back of a woman. One version portrays the scene at a crazy tilt. Another moves in tight on the same scene, so that the two figures fill the frame.]*

Katz: [pointing to the tighter version]: Yeah, that's very strong. It's close enough in that you can see the two live figures against the background of all the neatly lined-up and framed snapshots in the background. What is it you like about this one? *[She gestures to the tilted frame version.]*

Lee: The tilt . . . it's funny. It's extreme.

Katz: Print them both up and let's have a look at them on Tuesday. *[A stronger, darker image catches her eye. It is of a woman's face, pinioned under a man's shoulder. The woman's hand shoots toward the lens.]* This one, what about this one?

Lee: Yeah . . .

Katz: It's very strong. Try printing it, too.

Lee also submits these works-in-progress to a class critique. After they have had a chance to look over each other's work, each student moves to a new seat and is assigned the job of critiquing someone else's work, choosing the "strongest" image for a full-class critique the next week.

When Tuesday comes, the students talk about each image in turn, going over what they see, asking questions of the photographer, raising possibilities for what might happen as work continues. They turn to Lee's work.

Katz: Who put up this one of Lee's?

Shanette: I did.

Katz: How come you chose that one?

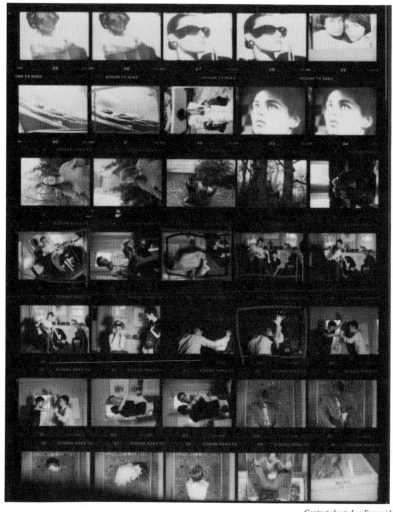

Contact sheet: Lee Fearnside

Shanette: I like the way it's on the diagonal.

Katz: What's that make it do?

Shanette: It makes it look comic. Like it's slipping, falling off.

Katz: What about the poses?

Shanette: They're ridiculous, out of a TV comedy.

Adam: "I Love Lucy," or something. "Saturday Night Live."

Katz: Everything in the image adds to what Lee is trying to communicate. The position of the camera, the position of the people in the frame. His expression. Her expression. What about the light?

Liza: The shadow. *[She gestures toward the man's shadow that looms on the wall behind his nonchalant figure.]*

Katz: Yes, look how much larger the shadow is than he is. What else? Look very carefully at the light. Where is it coming from?

Shanette: Here. *[She points to the upper right corner.]*

Katz: What do you notice?

Lee: You can see the light hanging into the picture.

Katz: I don't know if you were conscious of that, or wanted that. I have a feeling it might have been a mistake. But now it's a choice. You can crop it out or keep it. For me, given the made-up quality of the whole image, I like it. It's honest to see the light there. What kind of photograph does this remind you of? Where have you seen images like this before?

Liza: Old movie theaters, like in the glass cases.

Katz: Film stills. Whole scenes, all set up, with this white edge around them. Whether Lee meant to or not, she is touching off expectations, buying into a certain part of our experience with images. The format, the scale, the contrasts of this photograph all say, "Think scenes. Think movies. Think set-up comedy about men and women." But the tilt and the exaggeration, they say, "Think again." Very nice.

This "crit" session is a moment in a much longer process in which a teacher has been shadowing a student, setting up situations, writing comments, having conversations, all designed to urge investigation and the pursuit of visual ideas. But it is a fragile process, one that can veer between discussing and imposing ideas. As Katz says:

> This business of going public with standards is difficult. You want to teach your students how to think and work as photographers, not how to think and work like you. Lee's classmates endorse the droll side of her work. I see it differently: I want her to go for that strange, staged, ritual quality. And when I see it appearing, even by chance, I just blurt out what I see happening. To do it right, you

have to be bold, but in a way that leaves them room to think. It's like the light hanging down in Lee's photo. It was an accident, invisible. But you notice it, and hold it out, saying, "*See* this."

Lee Fearnside

Katz has a message: No amount of darkroom work will produce startling images where there was no visual investigation. No amount of mounting and framing will produce a project where a compelling visual idea wasn't present. It is easy to teach the practices of focusing or printing. It is much more difficult, but just as essential, to teach something about pursuing the standards of good work. ■

CHAPTER 3

A Chorus of Opinions: Classroom Discussion as a Focus for Judging Work

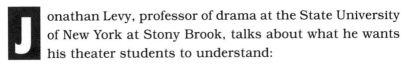 onathan Levy, professor of drama at the State University of New York at Stony Brook, talks about what he wants his theater students to understand:

> Most of what students learn in school encourages them to generalize, to find the commonalities in a group of particulars and, from them, formulate a theorem (or syllogism or law), which will explain the behavior of that kind of theory in all circumstances for all time. In elementary school we read Grimm's *Fables*. In graduate school we learn Grimm's *Law*.
>
> The dramatic imagination works in precisely the opposite way. The point and focus of the dramatic imagination is *particularity*, both in instances and moments. The playwright's stock-in-trade is the telling word and the gesture he wants the actor to effect. Since the telling word may well be the one garbled, or swallowed, or unspoken, and since the telltale gesture may be the tiny one, or the unfinished one, or the one contemplated and not made, playwrights must become close observers of the minutiae of human behavior. They must become experienced at reading nuance and hearing the unsaid, in seeing depths in surfaces and—without the intervening verbal machinery of, say, the psychiatrist, which can bleed life white—in seeing the implicit in the explicit.

Levy wants students to understand that a play is a blueprint for a live event. Unlike a fable or a tale, it does not unfold "long ago and far away." It takes place at two o'clock in the afternoon, at the picnic grounds, with the smell of barbecuing ribs in the air and the tablecloth snapping.

Questions and Revisions as Forms of Assessment

All of Carolyn Olasewere's tenth graders have been raised on written stories and other texts, and all are ready to treat a play as a line of sentences, not utterances. When they think of dialogue, they think either of phone chats or the tale-bearing talk of television soap operas, not of the silences and murmurs that pass between Linda and Willy in Arthur Miller's *Death of a Salesman*. To change all that is no small matter. Olasewere is an English teacher, not a theater teacher, so she could lecture about particularity, she could write it on the board, or she could even get them to read and underline Levy's essays. And she could grade the work they do in the drama unit of her class, giving out 20 points for specific details. But Olasewere has a different method, carrying the dramatic metaphor into her teaching. Students in her class read, write, and perform in the public theater of the classroom. Like it or not, students hear the quality of their work examined and debated.

Olasewere plunges her students into this process by passing out a clipboard and asking them to write serial dialogues, with everyone taking a turn adding a line. Everyone has to fall back on what they know intuitively about the workings of spoken language. Much of the writing is reflexive, rarely more than chat or spat. But Olasewere finds what she needs. Among the dialogues turned in is one about a man and woman confronting each other at a construction site, where she's the boss and he's the employee.

Olasewere provokes talk about the piece, pushing along the observations and questions with her own:

Olasewere: Okay, you are walking down the street and you hear these people. Why are you going to hang around and eavesdrop on their conversation?

Eesha: No conversation. She's mad. Like she's gonna kill him.

Jauneline: Yeah, a big fight's coming on.

Olasewere: Like a fist fight?

Marcus: No, words. Any time, they'll be shouting and slam-

8/88 Prod 2.

Setting: Construction site 2pm Friday
Characters: Rodger (employee), Ms Benson (Boss).
Relationship Boss- employee

Benson: Wilson get your behind
    over here!

Rodger: What do you want Ms. Benson
I am a little busy.

Mrs. Benson: When I say get over here,
    Snap to it.

Rodger: Who do you think you are?
I am getting a little tried of you talking
to me like a kid in the street

Mrs. Benson: You good for nothing wimp. As
long as you're my employee I'll say
anything I want. In fact, you're
suspended for the day. No money today, buddy.

ming things around.
Olasewere: Uh-huh, it'll get worse. Fast.... Anything else
going to keep you hanging around?

Jauneline: It's funny. She's the boss. He's supposed to mind.
Olasewere: Not what you expect.

By looking at a piece of student work, and asking them to imagine themselves on the pavement just next to the construction site, Olasewere is pushing her students to think about what makes a scene stage-worthy. They get several good possibilities going: they pick up on the instability of the shouting match and the switch in usual roles. But, even in these first days, there is a difference of opinion.

Veronica: Nobody that mad's gonna talk like that.
Olasewere: So, how are they going to talk?
Veronica: She's gonna sound good at the start. She's not gonna give it all away right first.
Olasewere: Be her.
Veronica [vehement, but cool]: Wilson, you *need* to see me. In my of fice .
Eesha [one of the dialogue's authors]: Uh-uh, no, outside. She wants it mean, in public.
Veronica: Why? There's nobody there.
Eesha: Yeah, the other guys on the job. They're hanging around on break.
Veronica: Not if you don't write them there. And he's not gonna say, "I'm a little busy."
Olasewere: Be him, then. I'll be her: "Wilson, you *need* to see me. In my office."
Veronica [mutters loudly]: "Yeah, what?"
Olasewere: Why that?
Veronica: He's not going to trust her. She's mean.

So there is work to be done. To give her students alternatives, Olasewere turns to reading short excerpts from published plays. These scenes are admittedly clipped out of larger works, but the point is to show students what can happen—how tension can mount, a secret can be revealed, or shared history can be disclosed in only 10 or 20 lines. Here is the excerpt Olasewere uses from *Member of the Wedding, by* Carson McCullers:

BERNICE: Come on. Don't act like that.

FRANKIE: *[her voice muffled]*: They were so pretty. They must have such a good time. And they went away and left me.

BERNICE: Sit up. Behave yourself.

FRANKIE: They came and went away, and left me with this feeling.

BERNICE: Hosee! I bet I know something. *[She begins tapping with her heel: one, two, three—bang! After a pause, in which the rhythm is established, she begins singing.]* Frankie's got a crush! Frankie's got a crush! Frankie's got a crush on the *wedding*!

FRANKIE: Quit!

BERNICE: Frankie's got a crush! Frankie's got a crush!

FRANKIE: You better quit! *[She rises suddenly and snatches up the carving knife.]*

BERNICE: You lay down that knife.

FRANKIE: Make me. *[She bends the blade slowly.]*

BERNICE: Lay it down, *Devil. [There is a silence.]* Just throw it! You just!

[After a pause Frankie aims the knife carefully at the closed door leading to the bedroom and throws it. The knife does not stick in the wall.]

FRANKIE: I used to be the best knife thrower in this town.

BERNICE: Frances Addams, you goin' to try that stunt once too often.

FRANKIE: I warned you to quit pickin' with me.

BERNICE: You are not fit to live in a house.

FRANKIE: I won't be living in this one much longer; I'm going to run away from home.

BERNICE: And a good riddance to a big old bag of rubbage.

FRANKIE: You wait and see. I'm leaving town.

BERNICE: And where do you think you are going?

FRANKIE *[gazing around the walls]*: I don't know.

BERNICE: You're going crazy. That's where you going.

FRANKIE: No. *[solemnly]* This coming Sunday after the wedding, I'm leaving town. And I swear to Jesus by my two eyes I'm never coming back here anymore.

BERNICE: *[going to Frankie and pushing her damp bangs back from her forehead]*: Sugar? You serious?

FRANKIE *[exasperated]*: Of course! Do you think I would stand here and say that swear and tell a story? Sometimes, Berenice, I think it takes you longer to realize a fact than it does anybody who ever lived.

BERNICE: But you say you don't know where you going. You going, but you don't know where. That don't make no sense to me.

FRANKIE *[after a long pause in which she again gazes around the walls of the room]*: I feel just exactly like somebody has peeled all the skin off me. I wish I had some good cold peach ice cream. *[Berenice takes her by the shoulders.]* . . . But every word I told you was the solemn truth. I'm leaving here after the wedding (act 1).

Events start in the middle. The talk is about unknown events; it is tight with innuendo. Students resist jumping in midstream:

"Who is Berenice? I can't tell."

"Is Frankie a boy or a girl?"

"I don't get what she means here. What's going on?"

But Olasewere is intent:

Slow down. There are clues. What is Berenice saying to Frankie? What kind of person would say that to her? There are clues. You tell me. You eavesdrop on people all the time.

She pushes them to use everything they know as conversationalists and listeners. Finally, Olasewere asks students to read the dialogue aloud as a way of proving their guesses about Berenice, Frankie, and the emotional traffic between them. With this assignment, students are thrust into performing. They have to raise their voices where Frankie is angry and petulant, they have to pause, swallow, or look out the window when her sadness and loss come to the surface. Several different pairs read, giving different versions of Frankie and Berenice. Olasewere picks out differences in the small, almost invisible gestures and contours of their performances:

> *Olasewere:* How come we have two different Frankies?
> *Eesha:* It just happened.
> *Marcus:* No, I think she was angry, she hated the wedding, or whatever it was.
> *Olasewere:* How can you tell?
> *Marcus:* The stuff she does with the knife.
> *Jauneline:* No, she's sad. Everyone's gone. She's left. The knife stuff is just covering up.
> *Olasewere:* Is one right?

From this kind of reading students take away a better understanding of drama as a kind of blueprint or score that can be played in many different ways.

Some weeks later, Olasewere ups the ante, asking students to turn some of their early dialogues into full scenes where "something happens between the people—not just chat." As these scenes are performed, Olasewere asks each student to take on one more role—that of the critic. Not the nasty, nit-picking kind, but the empathic, wise species who can see the kernel of an idea.

Alex, one of the original authors of the dialogue that took place at the construction site, goes back, revising and filling out the original conversation. After four revisions, he has created a moment with some of Levy's particulars: It is not *just* 2 p.m. on Friday afternoon; it's also hot. You can almost see the dust and frustration that hang over the gravel and the piles of lumber. The emotional heat is up, too. Rodger isn't alone when he is suspended by Mrs. Benson—he has been joking around with the guys. As he crosses to talk to her, they watch. And the situation he is facing as he walks isn't simple: he used to be Mrs. Benson's son-in-law.

The scene didn't come this far just through paper and pencil editing or contemplation. In part, it became as tense and as particular as it did because Alex moved from the roles of player-reader and playwright to the position of director. He cast two classmates as Rodger and Mrs. Benson. Then he chose

Alex Gordon
Working for a Hard Boss

Scene: Construction site 2 p.m. Friday It's a hot day and Codger,
Mrs. Benson's ex-son-in-law, is laughing and joking with his friends.

MRS. BENSON: Wilson, get your behind over here!

RODGER: What do you want Ms. Benson? I am a little busy.

MRS. BENSON: *[Shouting from her office door.]*

    When I say get over here, snap to it!

RODGER: *[All the men look at him and he's embarrassed.]*

    Who do you think you are? I am getting a little
        tired of you talking to me like a kid in the street.

MRS. BENSON: You good for nothing punk. As long as you're my
    employee you will do anything I want. In fact, you're
    suspended for today. No money today, Buddy.

RODGER: You think you can get away with this stuff cause
    you are a woman. *[Clenching his fists.]* If you weren't
    a woman I would knock that dumb look off your face.

MRS. BENSON: Just shut the door when you leave Rodger and you're
    also fired. You will receive your last check in the mail.

RODGER: Guess what? I'm already going to start a new job
    tomorrow.

MRS. BENSON: Just get out of my office Rodger now and I mean
    now! *[He laughs as he walks out of the door.]*

RODGER: Don't come crawling on your hands and knees ask-
    ing me to come back when this place comes down
    around that silly little head of yours. *[Smiling]* I'll call
    you; don't call me.

MRS. BENSON: I see why I never liked you. You're a brainless fool!

RODGER: Stop acting like a kid. What difference does it make
    if you like me? Grow up, I don't like you either, but I
    do my job. I won't work for you, ex-boss!

MRS. BENSON: Get out or I will throw you out myself!

RODGER: Real big ex-boss picking on a little employee like me.
    [Slamming the door hard and loud.]

another two and then another two. As he watched, he learned how he thought Rodger ought to stand and then cross the yard, and what Mrs. Benson might do as she hollered across to him. He heard Rodger's sentence, "I am a little busy," delivered in several ways—level, sneering, and fierce. Alex decided on the level version, so that Mrs. Benson's following shout could sound abrupt, and so that Rodger could be genuinely embarrassed in front of his co-workers. That way, Rodger's reply, "Who do you think you are?" could be indignant. As he worked through these decisions, Alex discovered implications as subtle as those that bind the steps of any argument or experiment. He sensed that there were many possibilities he hadn't thought of before. He saved them, marking his copy, almost as a musician might mark a score or a director might mark a script.

Several weeks later, a group of students read Alex's most recent draft. They caught the movement from joking, to surprise, to indignation, to fight. But they still had suggestions:

Jauneline: It goes too fast. I want to know what he did, just enough so I can tell how bad he really is.
Eesha: How come he already has a job all picked out? That doesn't go with him being surprised. Is he just faking?
Marcus: What are the other guys doing?
Jauneline: No, no—he could be in line for pay, and when he gets up to her, she starts in.

These student-critics go at the script, independent of Olasewere. They have begun to understand the way the particular details of speech and action work in theater. But, equally important, they have learned something about what it is to work as a critical audience. It inevitably involves a chorus of opinions—no two actors play Rodger the same way, no two readers appraise the text in identical ways. These students are beginning to understand that assessment is a matter of offering informed judgments, not simply a matter of marking the number correct. A student like Alex is being asked to do what playwrights do: read the reviews, think, and then make his own decisions. ∎

CHAPTER 4

Rehearsal as a Form of Assessment: "O Domine Jesu Christe"

yle Davidson, chairman of the Theory Department at the New England Conservatory of Music in Boston, talks about what he wants from a music student:

> I want a musician with a mind. Someone who thinks about when to breathe. Somebody who bothers to notice how another musician plays. I don't care if the person is going to sing, be in a band, play gigs, or listen to jazz in little clubs.
>
> And I'm convinced you learn to think as a musician largely in rehearsal—good ensemble rehearsal. A good rehearsal is really improvisational thought. The problems are unpredictable, the solutions matter, and they have to be worked out on the spot. To move toward a decent performance your attention is constantly moving from the whole ensemble, to a section, to the sound of an individual voice. You have to watch tiny details, like diction, build up into the larger issues of intonation and quality. All the while you have to shape the nuance that gives the entire piece expressive meaning. You have to be absolutely in the moment and thinking about where you are heading. You ought to be constantly reflecting while acting: "That was good. Remember that." Or, "Not the way to take that phrase."

Understanding performance

But it's not so easy to come by such full rehearsals. Each year, many school band conductors, orchestra conductors, and choral conductors are pushed to produce several large concerts and to enter many competitions. Every year they have to perform as much repertoire—or more—in as many parts as the year before. The press is for a note-perfect, technically impeccable, crowd-pleasing performance, not for students getting musical minds. As music teacher Linda Ross-Broadus says:

> I'd give up half the cantatas and half the four-part *a capella* spirituals for ensemble rehearsals where I could spend the time and take risks to get my students to think about their music. I don't want them just executing directions. I want them to listen to the different ways a piece might be performed. I want them to be able to step back and think about the quality of a performance. To argue about it. Giving students responsibility for judging their own work makes it possible for them to begin to think and work as musicians. They begin to be like the conductor, acting, but all the while making judgments and real musical choices.

Linda Ross-Broadus has taught choral music for more than 10 years. Like many choral teachers, her success, her enrollment, and her resources depend on the sleek performance of her ensembles at holiday concerts and competitions. But recently, Ross-Broadus has stepped back to ask what her students are learning from her as she rushes down the homestretch to perfect an upcoming concert. She has begun to ask if the rehearsal studio can be seen as an arena for "challenging students to think and solve problems in their own music-making, instead of always waiting to be told what do do." Collaborating with other teachers concerned about similar issues, she has reconstructed her classroom, opening up a dialogue about performance that continues from the first run-through, to a review of weekly rehearsals, to a fierce critique of any performance. This is not simply a matter of an occasional discussion. It has involved Ross-Broadus and her colleagues in a search for, and an invention of, a new set of classroom practices, ones that are aimed at making rehearsal a setting in which to think, choose, and reflect. Together with researchers interested in how students learn to think about music, these teachers have experimented with critiques, interviews, and conferences, all with an ear to insisting that their students become more than just the gears in a magnificent music machine. They want their students to become skilled

critics of their own work. These critical activities promote a two-sided conversation that takes place throughout the rehearsal process. Students are repeatedly asked to ask them-

---

selves, "What path do I want to take through this piece?" "What do I want to say with this performance?" "How does that single large decision affect the small details of the opening phrase, the flow of dynamics throughout the whole, the early and later rhythms?"

Preparing for an upcoming concert in which they will be performing Palestrina's "O Domine Jesu Christe," the chorus sings through the piece:

Ross-Broadus: Hear anything?

Soprano: The balance is off.

Ross-Broadus: Be specific. Tenors, what do the sopranos need to do?

Tenor: I think the bass needs to be fuller.

Ross-Broadus: Basses, were you listening to yourselves?

Bass: I think we missed the "p" on "potatum," measure 4, after A.

Ross-Broadus: But what about the intonation in the sopranos? What can you tell me about it?

Soprano: It was missing support for the pitch. We don't get under the pitch if we keep our heads up.

Ross-Broadus: Yes, that's the difference. O.K., let's tape it this time, and then we'll discuss it from each section's view.

The rehearsal includes not just direction and practice, but lively exchanges, structured and supported by the teacher, which occur when students participate fully in the rehearsal process. Students from different sections contribute their impressions of pitch, rhythm, and diction. Together, the ensemble and its conductor work toward increasingly specific critical judgments, which affect later rehearsals and, finally, the performance.

As members of the chorus, each of Ross-Broadus's students keeps a portfolio of his or her work. It includes sheet music marked with notes for performance, audiotapes made of successive rehearsals of the pieces they will perform, critiques of those rehearsals, and personal journals. The collection gives students the opportunity to develop a profile of their progress and accomplishments as members of a working ensemble.

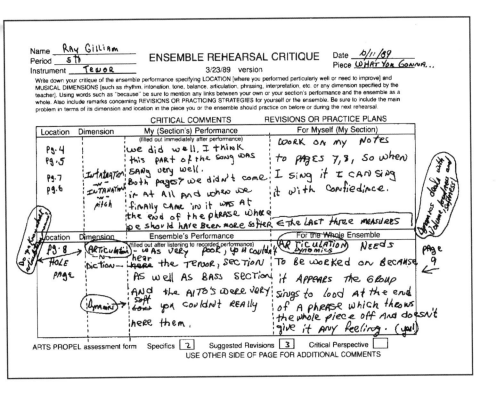

Raymont is in his fourth year of chorus. Like other members of the ensemble, he writes critiques of the group's performances. Although the idea of writing in music class seemed strange, the regular practice of taking a few moments at the end of rehearsal to set down his impressions has given Raymont the chance to reflect on the various aspects of choral work: diction, articulation, rhythm, dynamics, and stage presence. Even though he is still struggling with the difference between articulation and dynamics, he is beginning to understand something critical about the part-whole relationships within ensemble work.

Several months later, with continued practice, Raymont's comments become even more acute. Responding to the several separate dimensions Ross-Broadus has asked students to comment on, he describes the performance and his suggestions for practice with a much greater feel for the quality of the performance. He expresses his concern about the altos sounding "harsh" and the basses "chopping off the end of the phrase, which killed it." At least as important is the fact that Raymont sees the connections between these dimensions. He has begun to think relationally. He thinks aloud about how poor diction, for instance, can destroy the pitch, balance, and tone of a performance.

Ross-Broadus insists that her students see rehearsal as a place where they should be constantly noticing, making judgments, and raising questions. She asks her students to mark their scores, much as a conductor might, indicating trouble spots, not just for themselves, but for the choir as a whole.

These critiques are not private. Ross-Broadus treats them as much more than a record of an individual student's ability to listen critically. She uses them constructively, reading aloud from the most pointed and helpful, before she and the chorus begin the next rehearsal:

> At first, not everyone in the ensemble takes the critiques seriously. But once I begin reading aloud from them, they get the idea that I take them seriously. I even try using some of the practice strategies that students suggest. What eventually happens is that formerly silent students begin to challenge everything in sight—the seating arrangement, the way singers in other sections performed, my cues—all become fair game in their critiques. This shows me that they are not just repeating what I have taught them to say. They are integrating thinking and performance skills and taking them new places.

Eventually, this practice of critiquing permeates the rehearsal process. Ross-Broadus no longer passes out formal sheets; students don't have to write out their thoughts. Instead, she can call on their past work in thinking about performance:

> It is the opposite of the way I used to teach. I'd tell them everything that should be done and how to correct it. Sometimes, now, I forget and revert, especially if we are pressed, with a concert coming up. But recently we were having

trouble. I couldn't get a good sound from them. I went over and over the section, dictating to them. Then I remembered and I said, "Let's stop. If you were critiquing this, what would you say? What could we do to improve?" I gave them a few minutes, and then we went back and did the same section over again. The difference was phenomenal. They had engaged their own thinking processes, and they were problem solving. They were being musicians themselves.

The skills developed through this process stay with students, informing the way they listen to music and the judgments they make about other performing groups:

This past year, the Harlem Boys Choir gave two concerts locally and I took my choir to hear them both times. The first time we went, the students had had no experience with critiquing their own performances. Of course, we enjoyed the concert, but that was it. The second time, in between songs, they were saying to me, "Did you hear the intonation? Did you hear the diction?" It was as if I were standing beside other professional musicians.

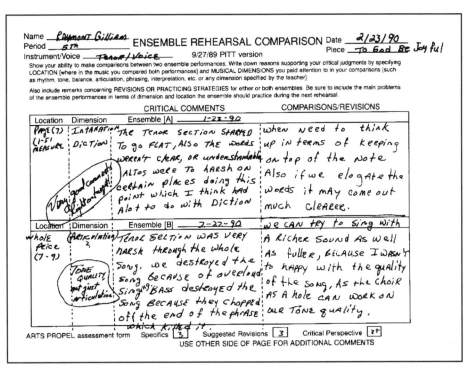

When they come to chorus, Ross-Broadus's students don't automatically pick up their music and file into their sections. Ross-Broadus and her colleagues have developed a range of practices designed to extend the thoughtfulness and responsi-

bility that take place during rehearsals into a wider, more thoughtful musicianship. Students interview one another, taking musical histories and talking about the place of music in their lives. They write in journals, keeping tabs on their own development as vocalists. On occasion, they move out into practice rooms to make individual or section performance tapes, which become a permanent record of their developing skills and musicianship. Though time is precious, even outright scarce, Ross-Broadus is struggling to steal or build moments when students can—alone, or with her—bring together what they know as singers and what they hear as critics.

But are Ross-Broadus's students learning anything other than how to talk a good game? Raymont and the other chorus members argue, "yes." Raymont says this way of rehearsing and listening has provided him with critical dimensions for improving his own musical performance:

> I've really improved my intonation in my quartet singing. Before, when Ms. Ross-Broadus told me I sang out of tune, I wasn't sure what she meant. Now I know, when I concentrate on my breathing, my diction, and sing out with confidence, I no longer sing flat the way I usually did last year.

And, as Ross-Broadus recalls, Ray is not an isolated case:

> When I found out that Ben—one of my best tenors—wasn't going to show up for our concert, I resigned myself to the inevitable balance problems in the performance. As it happened, I was surprised how well the tenor section did throughout the piece. After the concert, Eric, one of the basses, asked me how well I thought the tenors did. I told him I thought they sang surprisingly well. There was a big smile on his face. As it turned out, Eric switched to singing the tenor line during the entire performance. I was bowled over that he knew the music well enough to go from part to part. But more than that, it was his ability to anticipate and compensate for the balance problems of the entire ensemble that amazed me. ■

CHAPTER 5

Performance as Assessment: Making a Dance

aul Taylor, fresh from performing with Merce Cunningham, rushed home to try his own hand at using chance and experiment to choreograph dances:

> Curious, I went home and made several dance studies for myself using chance methods. After putting a number of steps in six or seven different random orders and then re-arranging the same steps in several other orders, both accidental and intentional, I concluded that a sequential order of steps, arranged either way, made little difference to the end result. What seemed more important than sequence was the type of step used, so I devised some combinations of movements by chance, both simple and complex. These all turned out not to be as unusual looking as one might expect and tended to look and feel very sticklike when executed—that is, without natural flow, muscular density, or sensation. It felt stingy, like something I'd not particularly like to do or see. And instead of being "abstract," as I'd expected, most of the movements looked like a wooden marionette having difficulty in expressing emotion. So much for making up abstract dances by chance, I reasoned (Taylor 1987, 47).

Developing a Critical Eye

In three widely dispersed classrooms, in three utterly different schools, three dance teachers have come to the same conclusion: If young dancers are to mature as artists, they must do more than perform as the neutral instruments of someone else's steps. They must become involved as choreographers, entering into the extended exercise of thinking that comes from taking a dance from idea through to the kind of demanding assessment that performance inevitably is. In the wake of this transformation in the usual dance curriculum, these teachers have also transformed the usual forms and responsibilities of assessment. Like Linda Ross-Broadus, these teachers insist that it is their job to teach students to be wise critics of their own work. And they, too, use the crucibles of rehearsal and performance. Each of them has designed a course to make this possible. One calls it Let's Make a Dance, another titles it, Making Dances, and, for a third, it is Dance Projects. But for Martie Barylick, Barbara Erlich, and Martha Armstrong-Gray, the impulse is the same: to teach students to assess their work and to make good use of their assessments.

In all three classes, the teachers have stepped away from an exclusive focus on the technical training associated with dance. It is not that they have abandoned issues of strength or of learning a dance vocabulary. Rather, they have chosen to transform students from neutral performers to active choreographers. As Barylick comments:

> Learning a dance technique does not, by itself, constitute dance education. Although students must evince technique to be approved as dancers in the adult world, technique is only one means to the art product known as dance. Learning only ballet, jazz, and modern technique is analogous to mastering "brush strokes" or "plaster mixing," without ever making a painting or a sculpture. Studying only technique keeps students in the role of "instrument." It denies them the role of "artist" (Barylick 1983, 120).

Consequently, in each of these classes, students take on dance projects, working alone or in small groups to compose, refine, and finally perform a piece of original choreography.

But something else gets invented, or resuscitated, along the way. It is an entirely different climate of assessment. In these studios, evaluation is based on a pattern of ongoing sampling of student work, rather than separate tests. Much as in an architecture class or a pottery studio, the teacher circulates, observing from the rim of activity. Where she senses trouble or admires a particular pattern or shape, she comments or raises questions:

> *Armstrong-Gray:* Okay, let's see what you've got. *[The students perform several phrases of their choreography.]*
>
> *Armstrong-Gray:* What holds the parts together? Why do you do those three phrases?
>
> *Student:* It goes to the left, then to the right, then in the center.
>
> *Armstrong-Gray:* Right. And it uses the space available to you in that way. That's good—it moves the shapes through the space. But watch in the mirror this time as you do it. *[Students repeat the phrases.]*
>
> *Armstrong-Gray:* What do you see? *[There is silence.]* It is exactly the same on the left, on the right, and down the center. You have to ask yourselves, "Why keep it the same?" Is this part of the dance about sameness, about uniformity? If not, what are you up to?

These conversations publish the dimensions and standards for "good dance." Choreography is not about filling up time and space smoothly. It is about having and embodying ideas about shape and motion. As Erlich explains:

> We begin all this by doing a group piece. I use it as a way of thinking aloud about making a dance. I start with what I call "abstracting a movement." You find something that is everyday and amplify it to make it dance. That presents them with the question, "What's the difference between an ordinary movement and an extraordinary one?" These students have done the basic vocabulary of dance, but this is to go beyond that, to do the work of giving expression to dance ideas. I'm an avid tennis player, so I worked off the idea of what it would be like to play tennis, but without a net. We worked with the basic movements of tennis, making sections, taking parts, talking about what makes movement interesting, and touching, on and off, on the larger ideas that could be caught up in those movements: singles, doubles, the boundary of the net, even when it's not up. But the point was to show them how to make a dance that was more than a collection of steps. Yes, to show them how to find the essence of what it means to move in that

way, and to make it larger and more extraordinary. To make an idea physical.

Implicitly, these conversations teach students what questions to ask of their own evolving performances: Is there an idea? Is it a movement idea? Is it made physical in interesting ways? In this way, assessment based on performance becomes an essential part of work—it is woven in as surely and as regularly as warming-up.

About once a week, as groups of dancers begin to work on pieces, Erlich calls for a "progress check." The clusters of dancers move through their dances as far as they have gotten, or select a particular section where they are stuck and want help. But whether they dance a whole piece, or some segment of it, the atmosphere and intensity is that of a real performance: dancers take the middle of the floor, nondancers sit as an audience, and silence reigns. Sometimes, at the end, there are spontaneous bursts of comments, or a question. But more typically, once all the pieces have been performed, the choreographers slide to the floor, knees drawn up or sprawling, to talk about their work. There is an interesting pattern of expectations. The choreographers are expected to describe what they are after, to highlight where they think they have "got it," and to isolate the moments or issues they experience as problematic. Of course, other viewers have things to say. The lesson is clear: the rapt attention and risk of performance brings an intense awareness of what is right and wrong in a piece. It shouldn't be wasted.

In her class, Barylick has evolved certain improvisatory exercises that are devoted to honing a dancer's ability to see the dance she or he is performing. One of these exercises, "Store Window," is well worth describing in detail:

> The dancers in Carolyn Brown's company inspired the invention of this improvisation problem, which we christened "Store Window." Their exquisite articulation of shapes threw into dramatic relief both my students' usual inability to etch shapes in space and their habit of moving from blur to blur in order to "get somewhere." By contrast, Brown's dancers were somewhere at all times, the audience was able to grasp the whole picture at every moment, as if each

dancer were outlined in bright neon tubing. "Store Window" has the primary intent of teaching the consciousness of shapes and the making of them, but it also allows frequent role transitions from performer to audience and back again. In this way, the exercise provides practice in composition, since it builds understanding of the "stage picture" (Barylick 1983, 125).

What's more, students also get practice in incorporating reflection into the choreographic process, stepping out, midpiece, to view their peers.

To do "Store Window," each student must be prepared with a "shape": it could be one he has used in class before, one he is using in a dance he's working on, one that he saw his cat assume last night, one that he saw in the film we all viewed yesterday. One further intention in this exercise is to teach students the differences between modern dance styles. "Store Window," after seeing "Appalachian Spring," looks wonderfully different from "Store Window" after seeing "Sue's Leg" (Barylick 1983, 125).

Barylick's students demonstrate that exposure to such sophisticated, reflective practices makes a significant impression and shows immediately in their own work.

. . . At the simplest, each student is asked to stake out a small working space of his own and compose, in a few minutes, one shape—to learn all its details, every cell of it, and to practice it facing different "fronts," or directions. The teacher establishes part of the studio as a large department-store window and part as the sidewalk outside. To get outside, the dancers must walk around the window to the outside of the store (no exits through the glass); they may exit and spend time watching through the window whenever they wish. The first one to enter the window is the leader. She walks to anywhere within the window space and assumes her shape, choosing any front, holding it for any period of time, then walks somewhere else, "hitting" the shape again, holding it, and simply repeating this over and over. She has the opportunity to feel what her shape is like as a soloist in various parts of the window, and it gives the other dancers the opportunity to memorize her shape (Barylick 1983, 125).

Choice and Development in Preparing a Performance

Barylick allows her students complete control over the content of their impromptu choreography, rather than intervening with suggestions that might make the performance more polished or informed. Even early in their dance education, she wants them to have the "real" choreographer's experience of choosing and developing shapes.

> Whenever the others wish, they enter the window space and, in their own time and space, each walks, stops, assumes the leader's shape, holds it, walks again. Now and then, a dancer will leave the window and become a watcher: perhaps half are watching, half working; perhaps most are watching, and a trio is working. The decision to return to the window is the decision to change the course of the unfolding art work. Whenever someone in the audience is so delighted with a stage picture materializing before her that she wishes to call it to the attention of all the watchers, she says, "Freeze!" The dancers stop and hold the picture as the watchers absorb it, taking time, perhaps, to have a brief discussion about why this arrangement is arresting. After this, all clear the window, going off left or right. The first person to reenter is the new leader, and the improvisation progresses until each has had a chance to lead.
>
> Each leader, after she has "taught" her shape as performer in the window, is naturally one of the first to leave and watch, since what she is seeing is essentially her choreography. The elements of her shape dictate where the dancers will choose to walk, which fronts they will choose, how long they will hold the shape, with what effort they will walk and assume the shape. If the shape is wide and open, the leader may see paper-doll lines in the "downstage" part of the window. If it is closed and interior, she may see distant grouping and few faces. If it looks like a frame from an action film, she may see busy comings and goings, much like "stop action." If it is a gestural shape, she may see social groups with suggestions of relationships forming and dissolving. Whatever she sees, she experiences moments of empowerment as an artist, a maker of dances (Barylick 1983, 125-6).

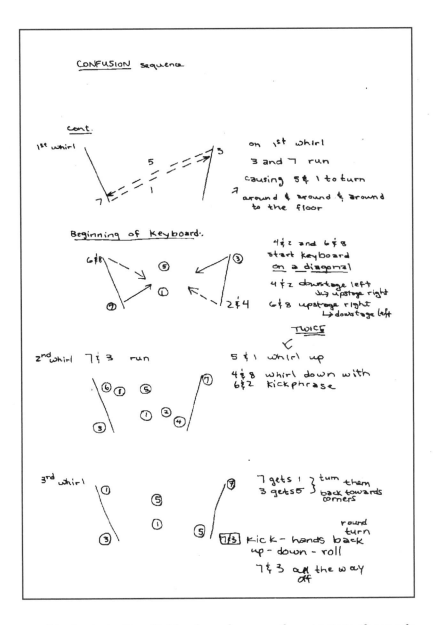

Students in Barylick's class do more than imitate the work of professional, experienced choreographers. They go through the step-by-step, moment-by-moment process of making a dance, learning what can only be learned by doing. But raw performance is not enough—Barylick also insists on the sustained performance of thought and attention. She requires, for instance, that her dancers keep notebooks in which they sketch out ideas for their dances and keep track of their constantly evolving notions of the shapes and patterns. When they moan and resist, exclaiming that "This is dance, not English," she is firm—they are "working on a dance."

The approach of an end-of-the-year concert provides a larger-scale form of assessment based on performance. In Armstrong-Gray's class, this takes the form of a two-day pause for assessment, which goes by the name of Selection Day. The idea is that each piece will be performed in front of an audience of other dancers who act as a jury. In fact, they score one another's dances, rating them on technical, choreographic, and musical grounds. Everyone writes notes to fill in where the numbers leave off. After each three or four dances, everyone stops, the sheaves of notes come out, and each dance is formally discussed: as a performance, as an idea, and as a spectacle (its lighting, costumes, and music). The question is posed, "Would you select this dance for performance? If not, what still has to change?" At the end of the day the sheets are collected into a giant notebook, organized by dance. Alone, or in performance groups, students collect their "reviews" and mull them over. With a week or 10 days still ahead of them, they plow what they have learned from Selection Day back into their work. What Armstrong-Gray and her students have invented is a set of practices that allows assessment to inform and shape final performances, rather than terminally judging or ranking them.

What all these teachers and students have invented is a set of practices that allow daily performances to inform final performances. ■

CHAPTER 6

Portfolio Assessment: A Gregarious Tradition

Walter Askin, a professor at California State University at Los Angeles, has this to say about how he tries to open up students' minds to art:

> Maybe the cruellest thing we do to visual arts teachers is to separate them from their studios. We give a chemistry teacher a lab or a vocational teacher a shop. What happens is that art teachers move further and further away from doing their own work. The students become their medium, and the teachers get better and better at designing assignments, prescribing the materials, insisting on the format. They end up stealing back from the students all the available choices. Teachers end up saying, "You need a little more blue in the upper left there . . . yeah, right there . . . a little brighter . . . right."
>
> But the best teaching multiplies and gives away choices in a kind of explosive way. You have to teach students that art is gregarious. Show them slides, send them to the museum, make them find out who else took on their problem. Talk to them about the ideas in art, and who had them. And then insist that the choice about the upper left-hand corner is theirs to make all over again, in good company.

The Autobiography of a Learner

In many visual arts classes, students keep their series of sketches and paintings in a portfolio. A portfolio of this kind makes public the autobiography of a learner. When the work in a portfolio is paged through, or spread out in its chronology, it opens that autobiography to examination and conversation. In this way, portfolios as a form of assessment are certainly part of Askin's gregarious tradition.

Ella is a high school senior who came late to the visual arts. But in Norman Brown's studio class she had long stretches of time to work, materials to explore, and the requirement to keep a portfolio that was more than an archive of her finished works. Ella's bulky portfolio contained a journal-sketchbook and the biographies of almost 20 works, grouped into several large projects or explorations. At the close of her second year, Ella and Norman reviewed the portfolio and talked about what Ella had learned about turning her ideas and memories into evocative visual forms.

As they begin, Ella remembers how she began making tentative, faint drawings that were more often only mementos or exercises. However, something important happened after several months of working in Norman Brown's studio class. She tried to make a watercolor copy of her mother's high school photograph. Her painting came out well enough, but when she tried to mount it on another background, it wrinkled. She cut out a frame in an attempt to conceal the mistake, refusing to give up. Ella—talking with her teacher Norman Brown—noticed and became absorbed with the antique, preserved quality of the wrinkled watercolor portrait, accidental as it was. Her stubbornness and interest in her mother's past began to take an intensely visual form. She stumbled on the connection between memory and its realization in color, texture, and surface. Looking back on that original drawing, Ella talks about how the experience with her mother's photo made her think about things she would not want to give up:

> I would say that after I started doing the pictures of my mother, it sort of started me thinking—maybe I could do a family series— not just my mother, but my grandmother and my dad and my cousin. And I think the whole series started from there.

She turned to an album of portraits she had made from photos of people she never knew or barely remembers; for instance, the "happy-go-lucky" male cousin who turned up smiling under a baseball cap and then disappeared. And there were sketches she made of her father. It was in those drawings that she began a struggle with the competing issues of realism and expression. She studies a drawing of her father holding her:

> I drew it pretty much as his likeness—his high cheekbones, his Indian part of him—and I like that. But here, where his arm is coming around my waist, I felt that I didn't draw the arm right. But I changed my opinion of it when we talked about Matisse in class, and I saw pictures in art magazines where the arms are somewhat distorted. My dad is just like that arm. I mean, he's really protective. And when I was growing up, he was with me a lot. I mean, he

Ella Macklin: Portrait of her father

wasn't the kind of father that says, "Go play, go play by yourself." You know, if I wanted to play, even though he was tired, he'd say, "Come here." I think that arm wrapping around me shows his personality, his character, a lot.

This conversation with published artists, and the kinds of talk that occur in the studio around her, changed Ella, forcing her to think about her right to extend and alter what she literally found in the family photos. When she took up the work of drawing a portrait of herself and her grandmother, this became all the more evident:

> In my family photo album at home she's sitting on the couch in the living room, and the photo shows the whole living room. But I just wanted my grandmother and myself, which was the whole focus, the whole center of my piece. Here, even though in the photo my grandmother is in the living room, I decided to take the picture and put it in an outdoor setting.

Ella Macklin: Portrait of her grandmother

TAKING FULL MEASURE

Here, Norman Brown adds his own comments, bringing out the visual effects of the open, breezy space Ella drew:

> It gives a nice feeling, other memories, maybe of a picnic, or some other time. Did she take you for walks in the park? That may have been in back of it. And all those cool, even colors, the uncluttered space around the figures, it takes your eye right to them.

Ella picks up on his attention to the visual qualities of her drawing, exploring how the soft, curved shapes convey the shared intimacy:

> I think there is more to this picture, because you see the way my grandmother's body hugs me. I think the meaning here is strength; it's warm, it's caring. I think pastels help achieve that—they can be blended and they can be smoothed even. Or they can be left rough in certain areas, where you want it to be highlighted.

Ella stayed with the project of grandmother portraits and created a series that includes an image of her grandmother as a young woman, elegantly dressed and posed in a severe studio photograph. But in those drawings Ella began to take liberties: she turned the sepia of the original into the soft tones of a tinted image, using pale watercolors. Brown comments that the thin blurriness of the application makes him think of the elusiveness of memory. Ella's own recollections are triggered; she remembers how she resisted the bareness of the original photo, filling her re-creation with objects she remembers from her other rooms—a lamp that was her grandmother's, and a hanging plant she observed in the studio.

Ella pursued what she called "this family quality"—the intimacy caught in soft pastel shapes that surround and hug. Part of the intensity of the exploration came from an exchange with another art teacher. From her studio next door, Karen Price, a teacher keenly interested in offering students points of entry to what is often the unsuspected or unexposed richness of their heritage, had noticed Ella's family portraits. Their intimacy and imagery prompted Price to offer Ella a catalog from an exhibition of work done during the 1920s at the height of the Harlem

Renaissance: drawings, prints, and studio photographs quite like that of Ella's own grandmother. Leafing through that early work with her own teacher, Ella remembers the fuelling effect of those images:

> *Ella:* The artists in there, they tried to capture the fact of the family. They tried to show the black family, and basically did their drawings in a way that people could see the closeness, the family togetherness. And I like that, because I am close to my family. Here is one. *[She finds it in the catalog.]* See, it's a man holding his son, I take it. It's called Christmas, by Palmer Hayden; he was one of the Renaissance artists. See, the man is holding the baby just the way my mother's holding me, and my grandmother's holding me. You see those same kinds of things in my pictures.
>
> *Brown:* Were you kind of astonished to find that other people had used the same ideas?
>
> *Ella:* Yes.
>
> *Brown:* Did that have an effect on you? Did it make you appreciate what you were doing more, even more?
>
> *Ella:* Because someone thought of it? It really makes me feel extra special to know that an artist, like maybe over half a century ago, had the same feelings that I have now, here. Sort of a connection there, I guess.
>
> *Brown:* Endless, timeless. But then, how are you different, as an artist?
>
> *Ella:* Well, I found their colors to be kind of drab, and I try to bring colors that add life. And other settings, out of my time and my life. But, like them, one of the things that I tried to express in my work is that sense of family, that sense of togetherness, that emotional quality. And when I was looking in The Harlem Renaissance book, one of the artists, William H. Johnson, said that his aim was to express in a cultural way what he felt both emotionally and spiritually about all that's been saved up in his family of primitiveness and tradition. And, basically, I think the same thing could be said about my work. We're a family, we're

proud of our black heritage, of black traditions, and our culture. Basically, I think what he was saying is that primitiveness and tradition is—when you walk into someone's home, it is the way it is, and that expresses who they are.

Like Karen Price, Brown sensed the power of being a part of Askin's "gregarious tradition." He sent Ella and her classmates up the steps of the Carnegie Museum and into the galleries to look for their colleagues, other artists whose work shows that they have confronted the same kinds of visual questions. Not surprisingly, Ella went with portraiture on her mind:

> When I went to the museum, I'd been used to seeing pictures that have the eyes, the nose, the face—everything's there for you. What I've learned to like about pictures that are just simple and don't have everything there is that, when you look at them, you are able to bring something to them. For example, here I just have the eyes, the expressions on my relatives' faces, but I don't fill in the nose, the mouth, because you know there's a nose, there's a mouth. I think the eyes—they say that the eyes are the windows of our souls—because eyes give a different feeling.

The effect of the museum visit took root slowly. In the following weeks, Ella carved out a different approach to portraiture—one that was deliberately simplified, pared down to the essential shapes. When she lined up her cousins on the family couch, she drew them as if they were Giorgio Morandi's bottles or Milton Avery's boulders—a cascade of overlapping shapes. The eyes were only accents, capturing the individuality of attention, silliness, or a serious stare.

The visit made her question the particularity of the images she had been making for months:

> I was tired of doing my family . . . because I want my work to be something that everybody can enjoy. I'm sure that if people looked at my art work, they'd say, "Oh that's beautiful, that's nice, but it's your family. What can I see in it for myself?"
>
> When I went to the museum, one of the things that I noticed was that the paintings, and even some of the sculptures, didn't have a face . . . so I could interpret it, I could

Ella Macklin: Portrait of figure holding a young child on a swing

TAKING FULL MEASURE

put myself into the picture, I could put in my own feelings.

Ella's first experiment after the museum visit was a much revised portrait of a figure holding a young child as they swing:

> This began the universal series that I later developed in which you have an adult holding a child, a mother holding a daughter, whoever. It happens to be my mother holding me on a swing. And I wanted it to be where anybody could look into the picture and see their own mother holding them, having fond memories of their own childhood. I didn't want to put in any features because then it would be, ". . . my family and not yours." I wanted anybody to look at it and have the same feeling.

But the effect of the museum visit was, ultimately, radical. Ella remembers encountering Alberto Giacometti's sculpture, *Walking Man*:

> He didn't have a face really, sort of an indication of a nose, or something. It could be any man, anybody struggling. It looked like a very struggling piece.
>
> *[She reads from some notes she made in the museum.]*
>
> In *Walking Man*, the figure of the man appeared to be held back as his back foot tried to advance forward. Basically, what I was saying is, if you notice, at the museum, in Giacometti's sculptures the back foot appears to be stuck in something. And he's leaning forward, he's trying to get away but something is holding him back. I think, the fact that Giacometti didn't put in any features, that is, in the face, could mean that it is anybody who is trying to get away from something, trying to advance forward in life. But something's holding them back.

Ella's growing awareness was also stimulated by the work of other students in the studio. A number of them had packed away their drawing materials and had begun working on plaster sculptures. She was taken by the stark, simple forms they were producing. After playing with pipe cleaners at her kitchen table she began sketching attenuated figures. She then moved to plaster sculpture herself:

> I was trying, looking for something that could still keep that family quality, but make it universal, so that every-

body could see a part of themselves in it, instead of just my family. And I'm sitting there with pipe cleaners, just twisting and twisting, making little figures. I originally had five figures, but I narrowed it down to two. And I said, "Well, going on with that family series, I could do a mother or a father holding their child."

I liked the way the quality of Giacometti's *Walking Man* was rough; it was a very rough bronze statue. And I attempted to create that same roughness. Even though you have good relationships with your parents, you still have arguments. You have rough edges in a relationship. So I left that rough quality. Because to smooth everything would be very unrealistic.

That rough quality started off as a mistake, because I originally wanted it to be silver smooth. But then I thought, "Wait a minute, life isn't like that. Not everything in life is totally smooth. Your best relationships, as I said before, can be rough at times." So, that's what I like about it. I tried to show the very fact that he's holding up the child. Lots of times you see parents walking with their children, down by their side; they're taking the children by their side, and it's sort of pulling along the child in life. You're taking the child everywhere you want to take the child. Here I think the figure is lifting the child, saying, "Hey, I'm trying to get you up in life. I'm trying to make you be better than I was." So I think it has a lifting-up quality.

Before Norman Brown began working with his students' portfolios, he kept a point system: so many points for attendance, so many points for completion, and so many points for good work. Struggling with the mathematics involved in the point system was easier than wrestling with assigning a number to stacks of sketches and finished works. But more recently, he, Karen Price, and other teachers decided to claim the tradition of portfolios, and to find some systematic and informative way to read and assess the autobiography that is evident in their students' work. Using portfolios like Ella's, they have thought through the major dimensions of strong artistic work with students. Now, students and teachers use this common language to review and evaluate work.

Reviewing Portfolios

But any system of assessment is more than the tasks it sets, or the dimensions along which performances are evaluated. It also involves a network of practices that turn it either into an exercise or an episode of learning. Consequently, teachers like Norman have grappled with how best to use their reviews of student work, and their resulting assessments. From the very first class, the teachers talk with students about these dimensions— much as Cynthia Katz does in her photo classes. With each project, there is a critique, where students talk about their own work and that of others, using these dimensions. Norman then grades and comments, using these dimensions as touchstones. At the end of a course students prepare a portfolio, and into that portfolio they place a collection of work that includes a statement about the work they have accomplished, a number of finished pieces to demonstrate the breadth of their work, as well as several biographies of work. These biographies document the progress of a particular piece, from early sketches through completion. Students prepare their own assessments of the completed portfolio, as do teachers. In conference, they discuss what each has noticed, where they agree and disagree. Their conversations have the sound of Ella and Norman. While they evaluate the work in the portfolios, they also talk about moments of understanding and about "pivotal pieces," where students came to realize a new idea or reached a different level of excellence.

ARTS PROPEL:
Process-Folio Assessment—Visual Arts

I. Production

    A. *Craftsmanship:* Evidence of skillful and appropriate use of materials.

    B. *Understanding:* Depending on the nature of the project, this may include (but is not limited to) the following:

        1. Demonstrated understanding of elements and principles of design;

        2. Rendering skills as demonstrated in such things as the ability to make recognizable imagery, appropriate use of perspective, etc.;

        3. Composition—centered, balanced, etc., as appropriate.

    C. *Inventiveness:* Evidence of creative ideas, strategies, or solutions to class assignments, and/or the ability to develop original projects. This may include (but is not limited to) the following dimensions:

        1. Originality of idea;

        2. Experimentation with imagery and materials;

        3. Risk taking—pushing beyond limitations;

        4. Divergent thinking—exploring unusual and diverse solutions to problems.

    D. *Commitment:* Ability to pursue an idea, problem, or expressive concern deeply and thoroughly, including (but not limited to) the following dimensions:

        1. Problem solving through multiple drafts and/or significant revision of work;

        2. Degree of time and effort put into work;

        3. Ability to complete work.

    E. *Expression:* Evidence in the work of expressive content, feeling, or mood. This may include (but is not limited to) the following dimensions:

        1. Degree to which the work reflects the student's personal involvement in the subject matter and/or project;

        2. Degree to which the work is expressively evocative, powerful, moving.

II. Reflection

    A. *Sense of self as artist:* The ability to articulate one's own artistic goals and working strategies and to assess one's strengths and limitations.

    B. *Critique:* The ability to articulate and defend perceived strengths and weaknesses in the work of others.

    C. *Ability to make use of feedback*—including the ability to incorporate new ideas or to disregard suggestions that are not in service of his or her work.

III. Perception

    A. *Ability to discern qualities in the work of other artists.*

    B. *Visual/sensory perception of the environment*—including both the natural and the human-made world.

    C. *Cultural awareness*—including awareness of the domain, familiarity with other related aspects of contemporary American culture, and awareness of other cultures, past and present. ■

CHAPTER 7

Assessment as an Episode of Learning: Beyond the Arts

Any assessment publishes a model of mind. The many short-answer questions of a standardized test promote a concept of the mind as efficient, encyclopedic, and untroubled by ambiguities. The message carried by the notebooks, journals, and portfolios of these arts classes is quite different. These forms of assessment insist that what matters is sustained thoughtfulness: the capacity to do as the photographer, Man Ray, insisted—turn information into inspiration.

Underneath this broad message, the forms of assessment discussed so far carry three essential lessons about monitoring or measuring student learning. These are lessons about the contents, the conduct, and the tools of assessment.

■ *The contents of assessment:* The assessments that Linda Ross-Broadus or Martie Barylick conduct could not take place unless they had reconceived what it is they mean to teach. Each of these teachers has moved from particulate exercises toward large projects, which demand that students take on the kinds of noisy and ill-defined problems that confront mature dancers and vocalists when they set their minds to the work of choreography or a searching performance of a musical piece. Given this framework, the contents of assessment have expanded to include more than the quality evident in a final piece or performance. No one is suggesting that final work shouldn't be handsome, well crafted, and precise. Rather, teachers have come to recognize how important it is that everything from their off-the-cuff comments to their semester-end grades address the full range of what is involved in *making* a work. Teachers like Norman Brown and

Karen Price have turned their attention to the way that students like Ella create a *body of work* over time—finding imagery that absorbs them, sketching and revising to find the forms and materials that are the right crucible for those images, searching books and museums for artistic colleagues who have worked in what Walter Askin called the same "gregarious tradition." They also attend to the growing reflectiveness and search in a student's work. On the pages of Ella's sketchbook, Norman Brown comments on her ruminations about an artist's right to invent, rather than just report on, reality. Paging through her collection of family portraits, he talks to her avidly about what he calls her "pivotal pieces," singling out the wrinkled high school portrait of her mother as the first moment when she understood how the images were memory and how the very surface of the watercolor sketch could evoke the age and haze of memory. He can't resist talking about what's invisible but everywhere present in her portraits: her effort, her willingness to revise, her capacity to use the critiques he and other students offer. *Assessment in these classrooms is based on complex problem solving, and so it is quite deliberately multidimensional— teachers want students to know how complex a thing quality is, and how long it may be in the making.*

■ *The conduct of assessment:* In each of the classrooms described here, an environment of assessment, rather than testing, is established. In this sense, assessment is a matter of the *ongoing* monitoring of progress and quality. Daily and weekly, students and teachers discuss images, the possibilities in scenes, or the realization of dance phrases in performance. So it is that Carolyn Olasewere's students debate the lines in a scene, or Martie Barylick's dancers decide which movements in their exercise of "Store Window" are worth saving. But students have to do more than listen to and absorb critique. To engage in these moments, students, not just teachers, have to take an active role in asking about the quality of emerging work and the standards that allow them to form judgments. So it is that Lee gradually finds the edgy humor for her domestic photographs or Ray refines his voice as a tenor. *In these classes, assessment is not a terminal occasion for grading or ranking. It is conducted, instead, as an ongoing episode of learning in which students are active participants.*

■ *The tools of assessment:* Given such a different curriculum and so diversified a notion of what is to be assessed, it is not surprising that the tools of assessment found in these classrooms are distinct. In place of multiple-choice-unit tests or end-of-course exams composed of short-answer questions, students like Lee, Alex, and Ella are constantly making biographies of works, saving notes, drafts, and critical responses. Barylick's dancers keep notebooks and Ross-Broadus's chorus members review last night's performance. In effect, all of these students are forming what could be called process-portfolios—longitudinal histories of themselves as people learning an art form. These process-portfolios are distinctive tools for assessment. They are not curriculum-independent tests of general achievement, they are rooted deeply in what students have been learning. They depend on direct samples of the processes and knowledge of value, rather than on indirect and artifactual formats like multiple choice, matching, or timed writing to someone else's prompt. They are based on long-term projects rather than on 40 minutes of work. *In short, as assessment tools, journals, critiques, and portfolios are designed to insist on sustained work and reflection, rather than cramming, speed, or sheer recall.*

But can these lessons about the contents, the conduct, and techniques of assessment translate to subject matter radically different from the arts? What would they look like? And what would they yield?

The Pursuit of Mathematical Power

Nanette Seago teaches mathematics. At the core of her work is the effort to prepare a wide range of students for the kind of mathematical work that demands much more than number knowledge and calculation. Like many of her colleagues in the California Mathematics Project, she wants her students to achieve "mathematical power," that rare combination of the conviction that they are mathematicians and the understanding that mathematics is a powerful tool for solving significant human problems (National Council of Teachers of Mathematics 1989; Romberg, 1992).

Surprisingly, for those who would make the case that the arts and mathematics are widely separate cultures, Seago's classroom is remarkably close to that of Cynthia Katz or Carolyn Olasewere. Her approach to assessment is strikingly similar to that of Linda Ross-Broadus or Karen Price, and she bases her assessment on portfolios.

■ *The content of mathematics assessment:* As she puts it, Nanette Seago "has left the book." Rather than plowing steadily through the assigned mathematics texts, chapter by chapter, she teaches a series of topics in mathematical investigation that are not unlike Cynthia Katz's photo assignments. These topics have to do with broad and powerful mathematical ideas like units, change, and probability. Embedded in those topics are traditional mathematical skills and procedures: a class session on fingerprints requires that students learn to use Venn diagrams to organize their data and then to argue for how many basic types of prints there are. Like Cynthia Katz's photo students, Seago's students work on these topical projects—like the fingerprint investigation—over a period of time, discussing the problem, generating data, presenting and critiquing solutions. Each week, on their own, students do "the problem of the week," an independent investigation where they have to apply what they have learned in a new context. Through these methods, the curriculum becomes a series of occasions on which to tackle large, messy, open-ended problems that do not give way to routinized solutions. And given the demand and frustration of what she asks, Seago offers her students models and colleagues. Just as Katz introduces her students to the work of adult photographers as company in the difficult business of visual projects, Seago teaches the human face of mathematics: how many people contributed, how much borrowing went on, and how much time it took to find certain solutions.

■ *The conduct of mathematics assessment:* Seago's assessment of mathematical learning is surprisingly close to what goes on in choral rehearsals or the long-term development of theater pieces. She has turned mathematics assessment on its side, looking for understanding rather than just answers. In so doing, she has turned her own attention, and that of her students, away from the bottom line and back onto the problem. For example, she insists—much to the students' initial surprise—that they justify their answers in writing. When they do "the problem of the week" they must show their work, diagramming or describing how they organized their data, how they worked the solution, and how they knew they had arrived or hadn't arrived at a solution. In turn, she writes comments on their work. Those comments draw attention to calculation errors or confusions over the question that was posed. But they also alert her students to other dimensions of mathematical work: the elegance of an approach, the wise use of resources, their ability to make connections across mathematical topics, or even plain persistence across trial and error investigation.

■ *The tools of mathematics assessment:* Given this view of mathematics, Seago wants to be able to look at how a solution evolves and how a student develops as a mathematical thinker. Like any mathematician interested in change, she needs samples of work over time. If she wants to observe many dimensions of mathematical growth, she needs "thick" samples that enable her to look for many aspects of mathematical performance: good questions, persistence, and elegance. Finally, as a part of becoming strong mathematicians, she wants her students to understand their own problem-solving strategies. So she wants reflection as much as production.

The result is that Seago, along with many of her colleagues

in the California Mathematics Project, has radically shifted the tools she uses to assess mathematical learning. She has shifted away from individual homework assignments and chapter tests. Like Norman Brown and Karen Price, she has turned to portfolios.

These portfolios are not quiet archives. Instead, they are live and changing data bases or evolving autobiographies of young mathematicians. The opening pages contain pencilled entries about their own mathematical careers and their personal definitions of mathematics. Like a series of footprints, the students make a chronological collection of their classroom investigations and their "problem of the week." But Ms. Seago regularly asks students to reenter and disturb the geology of what they have done. Like Linda Ross-Broadus, Seago sends her students back to their portfolios, asking them to reflect on what has proven hard or easy, what they have learned, or what still puzzles them, and to write it down. Even more surprisingly, she regularly asks them to return to a problem they have already done and do it again, comparing the two solutions. Sometimes she discusses what they have noticed in comparing the two solutions and sometimes she insists that they investigate and summarize the evidence of change.

The portfolio work is new and it is time-consuming, but Seago says she "wouldn't trade it in." When asked why, she pulls out a thick, spiral-bound yellow notebook and says, "See for yourself." The portfolio in question belongs to Vira Lim, one of Seago's students last year. It opens with an entry from September, where Vira gives this definition of mathematics and this reaction to his first encounter with a sprawling, difficult problem of the week:

His early descriptions of class projects stick close to procedure, inferences, and summary findings. For example, his entries from the fingerprint project outline how the data were generated, what the predominant and outlier patterns were, and what the facts he took away from the investigation were.

By the time he attacks his third problem of the week, his entries begin explicitly to portray thought, possibility, and search. Problem No. 3 describes a metric clock, where 1 day = 10 metric hours; 1 metric hour = 10 metric minutes; etc. It asks, "What is the time in our system when the metric clock registers 4 hours, 5 minutes, 6 seconds, and 7 miniseconds?"

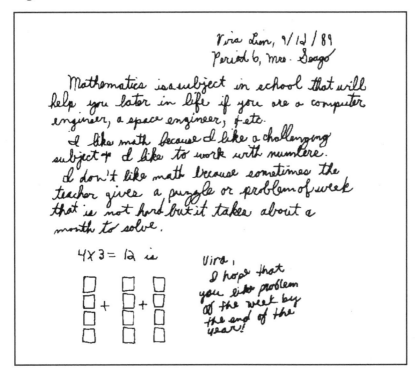

Vira's portfolio contains three pages of what he plainly titles *possible techniques*. Under this heading he embeds a diagram of a metric-clock face within the face of the conventional clock, carefully calibrating the unit measures on their rims to find his answer. On his cover sheet he writes, "I think the answer is 9:05:02 a.m., but I can be wrong. My research in the metric clock and drawing shows you, Ms. Seago, to see how I got my solution for this problem of the week No. 3. Also, my first page is kind of a data or headquarters of research."

In his note at the end, he comments on his discovery that his usual calculation strategies yielded to a visual solution: "I like this P.O.T.W. because it taught me to try many times to get

---

Oct. 3, 4, 5, 1989

Fingerprinting

We (our group) got fingerprints by scribbling on a separate piece of paper, and took tape and stuck it on our fingers to like copy our fingerprints. The majority of our groups + class was loops. I was the only one in this group with an arch.

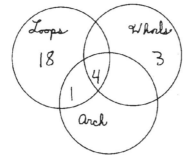

Key
L = Loops
a = arch
W = Whorl
LaW = ←
La —

Our class got 18 l, 6 lw, 1 la, 4 lwa, 3 w. We mostly got loops, and almost nobody got arches.

I learned that all fingerprints are not the same and there are three diffrent ways to identify a fingerprint.

the answer. It also taught me to look at a problem in a different way."

Partway through November, Ms. Seago asks her students to read through their portfolios and to reflect on what they notice happening for them as mathematicians. Vira writes about his changing feelings about the problem of the week: "I learned a lot in Ms. Seago's class. The first time I looked at problem of the week I didn't like it, but it looks better when you get it back and it says 10 + or Outstanding Work." But Vira goes further: "They taught me that patterns are helpful instead of doing it straightforward." For Vira, this chance to reflect on the course and results of his own investigations has turned up a math-

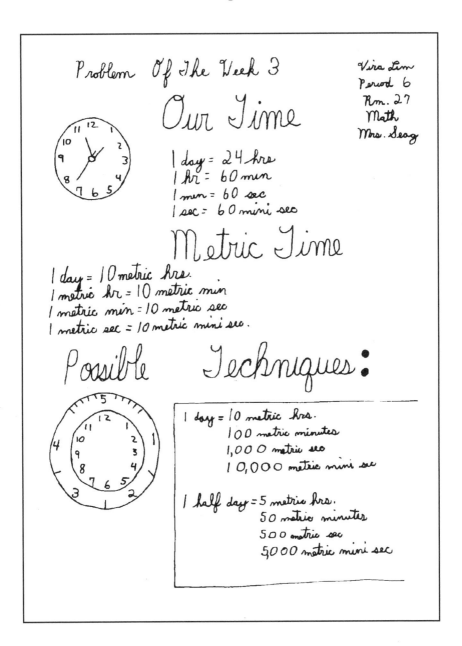

Problem Of The Week 3

Our Time

Vira Lim
Period 6
Rm. 27
Math
Mrs. Seog

1 day = 24 hrs
1 hr = 60 min
1 min = 60 sec
1 sec = 60 mini sec

Metric Time

1 day = 10 metric hrs.
1 metric hr = 10 metric min
1 metric min = 10 metric sec
1 metric sec = 10 metric mini sec.

Possible Techniques:

1 day = 10 metric hrs.
100 metric minutes
1,000 metric sec
10,000 metric mini sec

1 half day = 5 metric hrs.
50 metric minutes
500 metric sec
5000 metric mini sec

ematical idea—one that begins to structure and inform his work.

Problem of the week No. 10 is about the many ways in which a baseball team can win a championship series. It explains that to win, a team must take the best out of five games, and then asks how many different ways a team can win. It goes on to say that, to take the World Series, a team must win four out of seven games, and asks how many different ways that can occur. Vira's work is elegant. Borrowing from his own earlier idea of a data headquarters, he organizes his information. But this time, the organization is more than local. Even as he prepares the problem, he sets out to look for patterns. He specifies the possible cases ahead of time, realizing that the number of games played will vary, depending on what happens early in the series. He lays out these possible cases:

Case 1: 4 to 0 = 4 games
Case 2: 4 to 1 = 5 games
Case 3: 4 to 2 = 6 games
Case 4: 4 to 3 = 7 games

Then he displays his data for each case. In these displays, all the wins are entered as W. all the losses are entered as L. In his early efforts at this problem, he saw powerful patterns that he illustrates in this final display. He discovers that the winning team must always win the final game. He then lays out the patterns of wins and losses accordingly. He works out the patterns by beginning with the simple cases of straight runs of wins and losses, moving to alternating patterns. He also picks up on how the losses can show up in any of the positions in the left-right series. He underscores this by encoding the diagonal patterns of L's in red ink, drawing a blue arrow between them, to demonstrate what he calls in his legend, the "way of pattern." He then fills in the missing permutations in the total pattern.

Extension Problem X

Legend
W = win
L = lose

⌐ = a pattern
↘ = way of pattern

Part 1 3 out of 5 games
case ① 3 to ∅ = 3 games
case ② 3 to 1 = 4 games
case ③ 3 to 2 = 5 games

Part 2 4 out of 7 games
case ① 4 to ∅ = 4 games
case ② 4 to 1 = 5 games
case ③ 4 to 2 = 6 games
case ④ 4 to 3 = 7 games

① W W W

② L W W W
   W L W W
   W W L W

③ L L W W W
   L W L W W
   L W W L W
   W L L W W
   W L W L W
   W W L L W

① W W W W

② L W W W W
   W L W W W
   W W L W W
   W W W L W

③ L L W W W W
   L W L W W W
   L W W L W W
   L W W W L W
   W L L W W W
   W L W L W W
   W L W W L W
   W W L L W W
   W W L W L W
   W W W L L W

④ L L L W W W W
   L L W L W W W
   L L W W L W W
   L L W W W L W

   L W L L W W W
   L W L W L W W
   L W L W W L W
   L W W L L W W
   L W W L W L W
   L W W W L L W

1 W L L L W W W
2 W L L W L W W
3 W L L W W L W
4 W L W L L W W
5 W L W L W L W
6 W L W W L W W
7 W W L L L W W
8 W W L L W L W
9 W W L W L L W
10 W W W L L L W

On his summary sheet he writes:

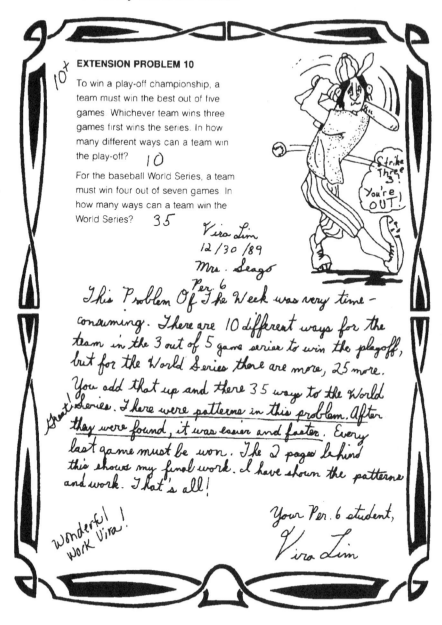

EXTENSION PROBLEM 10

10⁺

To win a play-off championship, a team must win the best out of five games. Whichever team wins three games first wins the series. In how many different ways can a team win the play-off? **10**

For the baseball World Series, a team must win four out of seven games. In how many ways can a team win the World Series? **35**

Vira Lim
12/30/89
Mrs. Seago
Per. 6

This Problem Of The Week was very time-consuming. There are 10 different ways for the team in the 3 out of 5 game series to win the playoff, but for the World Series there are more, 25 more. You add that up and there 35 ways to the World Series. There were patterns in this problem. After they were found, it was easier and faster. Every last game must be won. The 2 pages behind this shows my final work. I have shown the patterns and work. That's all!

Great!

Your Per. 6 student,

Vira Lim

Wonderful! Work Vira!

Even though Vira never fully explains what patterns he saw, the experience of uncovering the strategy of searching for regularities makes an indelible impression. In a later reflection, Vira chooses problem of the week No. 10 as his favorite problem of recent weeks, saying:

Problem of the Week 10 was very time-consuming. When I was done I could not believe the figures on my paper. I never knew there were that many ways to win a championship! I checked it over just to make sure, but it was still the same. Without patterns, this Problem Of The Week would have been impossible!

Like any other kid, I understood what math was, but when I went into Mrs. Seago's class I learned that it wasn't the only thing in math.

I chose this P. of the W. because one was very interesting and fun.

I learned that when you find patterns, you will be done faster and you will usually find the right question.

I liked this P. of the W. because it made me think more about the question.

At the end of the quarter, Vira looks over his portfolio and writes a new definition of mathematics:

Mathematics is ... not entirely multiplication, division, addition, or subtraction.

Mathematics is #1 thinking, #2 writing, #3 patterns.

#1. You have to think alot when you get an assignment in Mrs. Seago's class.

#2. In Mrs. Seago's class you have to write your explanation for your answer.

#3. Patterns make it easier and faster for you to get the answer (s).

CHAPTER 8

Testing and Assessment

The point is simple. In many schools throughout the United States, student assessment takes the form of testing. Many of the tests students encounter, by virtue of the tests' design as a series of unrelated questions, draw teaching and learning toward the mastery of facts and away from large ideas and processes. Students' repeated encounters with multiple-choice timed tests teach them that the bases for success in school are first-draft answers rather than sustained explorations, correctness rather than risk, and information rather than conceptualization (Resnick and Resnick,1991; Wiggins 1989a and 1989b; Wolf et al. 1991; Wolf, 1992). Our current modes of testing vest the responsibility for characterizing student learning far from the classroom. These forms of testing revoke from teachers and from students any substantial role in student assessment, since high-stakes decisions about promotion, retention, and students' programs lie with scores, rather than with clinical judgments. When this kind of testing becomes the major yardstick of educational progress, students are prevented from learning to take an active role in assessing their own and others' work. Students do not see their tests again, they do not have an opportunity to revise their work, nor are they asked to draw conclusions from the patterns of their performances. This is destructive, particularly if we want our students to learn how to become informed critics, capable of the choices made by Amalia Mesa-Bains, Paul Taylor, or Vira Lim.

The teachers and students described here—whether they are making music or mathematics—engage in a very different kind of assessment. In their classrooms, assessment grows out of public discussions of the dimensions of excellence. It is a matter of exchanging informed clinical judgments and uncovering overlaps of or tensions between opinions. It is not terminal, but ongoing. It requires students to take an active role. It occurs in multiple forms. Frankly stated, its purpose is not accountability, but learning (Stenmark 1989; Wolf, 1992).

Short-answer testing has become a habit. It is not a necessity. As the students and teachers here make clear, we are rich in alternatives. ■

REFERENCES

Barylick, Martha. 1983. "Both Artist and Instrument: An Approach to Dance Education." *Dœdalus* 112(3), 113–127.

National Council of Teachers of Mathematics. 1989. *Curriculum and Evaluation Standards for School Mathematics.* Reston, Va.: NCTM.

Resnick, Lauren. 1987. *Education and Learning to Think.* Washington, D.C.: National Academy Press.

Resnick, Lauren and Leopold Klopfer, eds. 1989. *Toward the Thinking Curriculum: Current Cognitive Research.* 1989 Yearbook of the Association of Supervision and Curriculum Development. Alexandria, Va.: ASCD.

Resnick, L. B., and D. Resnick. 1991. "Assessing the Thinking Curriculum: New Tools for Educational Reform." In B. R. Gifford and M. C. O'Conner, eds., *Changing Assessments: Alternative Views of Aptitude, Achievement, and Instruction,* Boston: Kluwer Academic Publishers.

Romberg, Thomas A. 1992. "Problematic Features of the School Mathematics Curriculum." In Philip W. Jackson, ed., *Handbook of Research on Curriculum.* New York: Macmillan.

Solotaroff, Ted. 1987. *A Few Good Voices in My Head: Occasional Pieces on Writing, Editing, and Reading My Contemporaries.* New York: Harper and Row.

Stenmark, Jean Kerr. 1989. *Assessment Alternatives in Mathematics: An Overview of Assessment Techniques that Promote Learning.* Berkeley, Ca.: EQUALS Publications.

Taylor, Paul. 1987. *Private Domain.* New York: Alfred Knopf.

Wagner, Catherine. 1988. *American Classrooms.* New York: Aperture.

Wiggins, Grant. 1989(a). "A True Test: Toward More Authentic and Equitable Assessment." *Phi Delta Kappan* 70, 703–713.

— — 1989(b). *Questions and Answers on Authentic Assessment.* Paper presented in October 1989 at Beyond the Bubble: Curriculum Assessment/ Alignment Conference, Sacramento, Ca.

Wolf, Dennie. 1992. "Assessment as an Episode of Learning." In R. Bennett and W. Ward, *Construction Versus Choice in Cognitive Measurement...* Hillsdale, N.J.: Lawrence Erlbaum Associates.

Wolf, Dennie, Janet Bixby, John Glenn, III, and Howard Gardner. 1991. "To Use Their Minds Well: Investigating New Forms of Student Assessment." In Gerald Grant, ed., *Review of Research in Education,* Washington, D.C.: American Educational Research Association.

Ybarra-Frausto, Tomás. 1986. "Maintenance and Extension of Traditions." *Lo del Corazón: Heartbeat of a Culture.* San Francisco: The Mexican Museum.

8107